SOUTHERNER

TAKE YOUR STAND!

Reclam Your Identity

Reclaim Your Life

JOHN VINSON

Foreword by Dr. Clyde N. Wilson

SHOTWELL PUBLISHING LLC

Columbia, So. Carolina

Produced in the REPUBLIC OF SOUTH CAROLINA by

SHOTWELL PUBLISHING LLC
Post Office Box 2592
Columbia, So. Carolina 29202

www.ShotwellPublishing.com

Cover design: Boo Jackson Designs.

ISBN-13: 978-0692623206
ISBN-10: 0692623205

THE SOUTH IS A LAND that has known sorrows. It is a land that has broken the ashen crust and moistened it with tears, a land scarred and riven by the plowshare of war and billowed with the graves of her dead, but a land of song, a land of hallowed and heroic memories.

— Ned Carmack

CONTENTS

FOREWORD

SOUTHERNERS ARE REAL PEOPLE. And we know who we are. Despite all the forces, both deliberate and unplanned, working to do away with us, we are still here. In fact, in an increasingly "diverse" society, we may be the largest group of actual Americans left in North America. And we can claim truly that we are a people who existed long before there was any such thing as the "United States of America."

A gifted historian once described the South as "not a nation within the nation, but the next thing to it." The South has long been defined as a deviation from the American norm. There are two things to be said about that. First, until 1861 the South was the American norm, while New England, for example, was known as a deviation. Second, exactly what is the American norm? The South has not so much deviated as just remained what it is. It has simply preferred not to chase the American norm because the American norm is a moving target. And never more so than in the past few decades. The South is changing but let us hope it will never change fast enough to catch up with the culturally and morally disintegrating society that we now live with in the United States.

Having been incorporated into the "union" against our will, and having been to a degree subjected to all the destructive forces loose in the Western world today, we Southerners have no institutions we can count on. We will have to order our lives in such a way that we can survive as a people and create sustaining institutions. With the eloquence of true patriotism, John Vinson herein tells us who we are and what we must do to remain so.

Clyde N. Wilson
Carolina, 2015

INTRODUCTION

THIS BOOK DEFENDS THE TRUE SOUTH, not the New South, not the Sunbelt. Its message is to that brave remnant of Southerners who are proud of their heritage and culture, men and women of distinction who are determined that their beloved Southland will remain a distinctive region.

The trends of the modern world pose many obstacles to this goal, but these same trends are all the more reason why the effort is vital and necessary. Today is the era of the "mass man," a creature so harassed and hurried that he scarcely has time to develop the values and quality relationships that alone give meaning and purpose to human existence. More and more, our modern society is one of big institutions, Big Government, Big Corporations, and little pathetic people. This is a dangerous situation if we, as Americans, truly value freedom. Founding Father Thomas Jefferson firmly believed that the Constitution by itself would not protect liberty if the majority of citizens lost their self-reliance and other traits of character we commonly associate with a free people. Jefferson, a Virginia planter, was a Southerner. So were most of the other prominent Founders, among them George Washington and chief architect of the

Constitution James Madison. Truly the roots of American liberty grew from Southern soil and Southern values. Even today this proud tradition continues. The Southerner, at least outside the largest urban areas, is not nearly so much the mass man as the common types in other regions. He remembers his ancestors, values religious faith, and harbours the instinct to rebel against arbitrary, oppressive rules.

Even so, the South stands at a crossroads. One fork leads to a "Brave New South" where old times, honour, and love are forgotten in a mad rush for consumer trinkets, status, and conformity. To ease the pain of this madness, people will turn ever more to the "remedies" of alcohol, drugs, and video fantasies. Sale of the Southern soul may bring a temporary prosperity, but as in any deal with the devil, the devil always comes to collect. The other fork is the path of the True South, a creative adapting of the Southern past and its sustaining values to meet the challenges and conditions of the future.

The Brave New South has powerful, wealthy advocates, both inside and outside the region. Contending against them will not be easy. Nevertheless, there is still that sizeable remnant of true Southerners who retain honour and self-respect; who have refused to bend a knee to the Moloch of mass society. Like the early Christian minority that overturned the might and corruption of Imperial Rome, they could present a potent spiritual force far beyond their numbers. The hope of this book is to rouse the Southern remnant and provide new ideas for action. The author sees Southern heritage resting on four pillars: culture, family/community, love of liberty, and love of the land. It will describe forces opposed to Southern heritage and steps true Southerners can take to thwart and defeat them. The cause of the South is no Lost Cause, but the cause of freedom and human dignity.

CHAPTER ONE
SOUTHERN HERITAGE

CULTURE

THE SOUL OF A PEOPLE and their region is their culture. With Southern culture, as with every other culture, it is the sum of all values, beliefs, ethnic character, history, tradition, and folklore that binds a people together, ties them to a particular place, and makes them unique.

Culture provides people identity, guidelines, goals, and inspiration. People who lose touch with their culture, such as some groups of American Indians, suffer high rates of suicide, alcoholism, and other types of personal and social breakdown. Culture is the sustainer of mental, emotional, and spiritual health.

What, then, makes Southern culture? Christian faith and belief in fixed principles. Faith is stronger in Dixie than other parts of the country. Our region is the "Bible Belt," a description no one would ever think of applying to the Northeast or California.

With faith goes the belief that right is right and wrong is wrong, and that the two are not just relative ideas. Polls show that Southerners are more traditional on many moral questions and values than the rest of the country. It was mainly Southern states which defeated the feminist Equal Rights Amendment to the Constitution after it went to the states for ratification in the 1970s. To Southerners, if God did not make Adam and Eve the same, then neither should the law. Critics say that strong views of right and wrong on personal morality issues (such as premarital sex, same-sex "marriage," and gambling) promote intolerance. Traditional Southerners just call it conviction and right living.

Southern Christianity is not the same as Northern varieties of the faith. The Old Testament has a stronger influence in Southern religion. The Old Scriptures say that the physical world, though fallen, is real, and (as the Lord said in *Genesis*) it is good. Passions and feeling are good, too. The *Psalms* and the *Song of Solomon* say so. As a consequence, Southern church people are not inclined to become so "spiritual" that they lose contact with the earth and common sense. This they leave to Yankee religionists and other "reformers" whose "idealism" has often taken flight from reality. The Southerner knows that heaven will never be on earth, and distrusts the "idealists" who try to bring it. Too often he's seen their "ideals" create hells on earth, as his ancestors saw first-hand between 1861 and 1865.

Comfortable with nature, the Southerner understands human nature. He understands it for good and bad, and accepts it. His Bible says that man hasn't changed in the past 5,000 years and even with Saving Grace human character won't change a great deal.

This is one reason sentiment for capital punishment is stronger in the South than in other parts of the country. The Southerner sees that some people are just no good because that is their nature. Nothing short of the electric chair will reform or rehabilitate them.

But attachment to nature and the material world do not make the traditional Southerner materialistic. He takes seriously the injunction, "What profits a man if he should gain the whole world, but lose his soul?" The South has always valued the intangibles of the spirit. The true Southerner will make money, but he will not make money his god. That violates the First Commandment. He values his leisure as a time to fellowship with his fellows and his Creator.

Cultivating the spirit, he is given to song and sentiment, shown even today in his Bluegrass, Country, and Gospel music. Once confined to the South, these musical forms have picked up popularity across the country and the world. By keeping the faith, the Southerner still remembers how to "make a joyful noise."

Family/Community

The long genealogies and family histories in the Old Testament help inspire the second pillar of Southern culture after faith: family and kinship. Southerners, much more than other Americans, know their roots and who they come from. Where a Californian may not know or care who his great-grandfather was, a Southerner will often be able to tell a listener more than he wants to hear. As a South Carolinian once observed: "One thing we have in common with the Chinese is that we both worship our ancestors."

A sense of who he came from gives many a Southerner a sense of identity. Unlike a lot of modern Americans, he does not need to pay thousands of dollars to psychologists to find out who he is. He already knows.

Some people, however, criticize Southerners for being too occupied with forebearers and the past, and not sufficiently engaged in the present. This can be a valid criticism. Yet it must also be said that we forget our past at our peril. People without memory of who and what have come before them lose the wisdom gained by past generations. They become self-centered and lose interest in what happens after them. Those who do not care for past generations, noted British political philosopher Edmund Burke, will not care for future generations either.

But Southern family ties are not just links to the past. Southern families today are more connected than elsewhere. The plague of divorce and single living has by no means by-passed the modern South. Still, Southern families hold sentiments and affections not so common outside Dixie. One small example: A large number of adult Southerners refer to their parents as "Daddy" and "Mama." In the South, a family name often carries a mystique—a source of memory and honour to uphold.

Certainly in the South the bonds of extended family are stronger than in other parts of the country. Southerners seem to know their uncles, aunts, first cousins and even second cousins—pretty well. And though it is hard to prove, it does appear that the region hosts more family reunions than other parts of the country.

The feeling of Southern kinship comes in part from Southern

origins. A large percentage of white Southerners came from "Celtic" lands such as Scotland where the tradition of clans and tight-knit families was strong. Some historians believe that this Celtic influence was one of the most significant influences on Southern identity. The cross on the Confederate battle flag is taken from the cross of Saint Andrew on the flag of Scotland.

During the War for Southern Independence, Southerners rose in defense of their homeland as a family more than as a nation. That conflict and "Reconstruction" forged Southerners as never before into a unique people. The South is a region with its own flag, dialect, cooking, music, literature, and special history. It is a history which lives in family memory.

LOVE OF LIBERTY

The third pillar of Southern heritage is love of liberty. As noted in the introduction, the leading architects of American freedom were Southerners. Virginian Thomas Jefferson wrote the Declaration of Independence, and Virginian James Madison was the principal author of the U.S. Constitution. From the beginning of the Union, Southerners have stressed the importance of personal freedom.

With their strong sense of history and tradition, these and other Southern thinkers searched the record of past civilizations—most notably ancient Rome—to discover what political and economic arrangements best promoted liberty. This study and the Christian view of man's sinful nature led them to conclude that power centralized in the hands of a few is a threat to freedom.

If those few go bad and do evil, no other power will exist to stop them or hold them in check. Freedom is most secure, they reasoned, when power is divided and held in balance among groups. This was the source of the "checks and balances" that Madison and other thinkers built into the Constitution. It provided for three branches of government—executive, legislative, and judicial—each with given duties and each keeping watch on the others.

Another constitutional facet of "checks and balances" was strong provision for state authority and power against the centralizing power of the federal government in Washington. For generations, Southern statesmen led the nation as defenders of "states' rights." They firmly believed that without states' rights, individual rights would have little defense against centralized power.

From the beginning of the American Republic to 1865, Southern political thinkers held that a state, in defense of liberty, had the right to break away from an oppressive central government. This was a common view among Northerners. In 1814, representatives from the New England states discussed pulling out of the Union as a result of a disagreement over U.S. involvement in the War of 1812. As late as 1848, a rising Northern politician conceded the right of a state to leave the Union. His name was Abraham Lincoln.

The Southern Founders never believed, however, that political arrangements alone were enough to guard liberty. Far more necessary was what Jefferson called "virtue" or the strength of character of the people. In Jefferson's view, if the people did not have the foresight and discipline to rule themselves, the morality to know right and wrong, and the courage to act on their convictions, they could never be an effective check against the ambitions of tyrants.

The development of those traits, Jefferson believed, required an economic system where most people were self-employed in earning their livelihood. When people work for others, he argued, they often do not develop traits of independent thought and action. Not accustomed to exercising liberty in their personal lives, they have little understanding of what political freedom is or how to maintain it.

As Jefferson and other Southern thinkers pointed out, a man who works for someone else is not always willing to speak his mind and act as he thinks proper. Always in the back of the employee's mind is the fear that if his speech or actions offend the boss or company, he may lose his job. Jefferson and the others would have had grave reservations about the prospects of freedom in a society where most people call someone "boss."

The South's love of freedom has shown itself in a long line of statesmen from past to present. From John C. Calhoun to the late 19th century Populists to Richard B. Russell and Sam Ervin, Southern statesmen have stood in the breach against centralizing powers, be they political or economic.

At the popular level, the good old boy flexes his freedom against bureaucratic conformity and the effeminate moralizing of America's trendy class. The rifle in the gun rack in the back of his pickup is not there for decoration. He uses it to hunt, as his pioneer ancestors did. The rifle is also a warning against potential tyrants. The good old boy may never have read the theory of the Second Amendment, but instinctively he understands it well. Armed citizens are a check and balance. As Thomas Jefferson pointed out, "The strongest reason for the people to retain the right to keep and bear arms is, as a last resort, to protect themselves against tyranny in government."

One more point to be made on freedom is to refute, briefly, the charge of professional South-haters that the Old South did not stand for freedom, but slavery. They allege that it was the cause for which the Confederacy went to war.

A few reflections on the past show this to be nonsense. Slavery came about during British rule. Southern colonists admittedly purchased slaves, but shipping and selling them were British and Yankee shippers. New England grew rich from slave commerce. Africans who enslaved and sold their fellow Africans supplied cargos for the slave shippers.

Following the American Revolution, sentiment against slavery grew in the South. Jefferson spoke out against it. By 1830, a majority of anti-slavery societies were in the South. Shortly thereafter, Virginia came within a few votes of abolishing slavery. In 1833, the British Empire peacefully ended slavery.

Certainly this could have happened in America. But it was not to be. Self-righteous fanatics in the North, the abolitionists, called the South wicked and demanded immediate emancipation, regardless of the consequences. As time went on some even urged a slave revolt and the massacre of Southern whites. Stunned and put on the defensive, the South dug in its heels, and the movement toward peaceful abolition stopped. No less a unionist than Daniel Webster conceded that the South might have ended slavery had it not been for the abolitionists' fanatical crusade.

In 1859, abolitionist John Brown was tried, convicted, and hanged after attempting unsuccessfully to incite a slave revolt in Virginia. He had the backing of powerful Northern interests and a significant body of Northern opinion hailed him as a hero. The next year Abraham Lincoln, a president identified with the abolitionists, came to power in Washington.

At this point, many Southerners questioned allegiance to a Union that seemed indifferent to their rights and even safety. Initially, the Upper South states of Virginia, North Carolina, Tennessee, and Arkansas refused to leave the union. The Lincoln government could have conciliated these states and perhaps defused the Southern independence movement. Instead, it provoked the Confederacy to fire on Fort Sumter, and then called for 75,000 volunteers to invade the South. Rather than participate in the invasion of their sister Southern states, the Upper South withdrew.

The motive for secession was not defending slavery, but defense against an aggressor trampling on states' rights and local rule—the same principles for which the American Revolution was fought. The South fought not to keep slavery, but for the right to deal with that institution in its own way and time.

If one believes that the Southern cause was preserving slavery, he has some difficult facts to explain:

1) Confederate president Jefferson Davis at the beginning

of the war said that slavery would not long endure.

2) The Confederate Constitution prohibited the importation of slaves.

3) Robert E. Lee turned down Abraham Lincoln's offer of command of the Union Army, to side with the South. Lee later took command of the Confederate Army of Northern Virginia and eventually all Confederate forces. Lee opposed slavery.

4) In 1864, the South proposed to European countries that it would abolish slavery if they would recognize the Confederacy.

5) At the Hampton Roads conference just two months before the war ended, Abraham Lincoln offered the possibility compensating Southern slave owners for freed slaves if the South would immediately lay down its arms. The South refused, preferring a nearly vain hope for independence over protecting the investment in slaves.

6) Three-quarters of white Southerners neither owned slaves nor were members of families that did. Throughout the war non-slave owners fought with utmost determination.

These facts, hard to fit with slavery as the Southern cause, are perfectly consistent with a South fighting for its principles and self-determination. If the South had won, Southerners sooner or later would have ended slavery. But this would have been a peaceful emancipation, unlike the one of deep suffering for both white and black and financial ruin forced by the North.

That bitter emancipation had much to do with long-lasting racial antagonism in the South. Approximately a hundred years after Appomattox, Northern politicians seized on those antagonisms to continue the centralizing of federal power begun by Lincoln. They claimed their brand of civil rights laws was the only way to end injustice to blacks. Jefferson would have seen an unchecked and unbalanced federal government as the beginning of injustice for everyone. Racial wrongs did exist in the South, but creating Washington Almighty was no answer. Centralized government and freedom simply cannot co-exist.

LOVE OF THE LAND

The fourth pillar of the South's heritage is love of the land. The soul of the South is rural and agrarian. Jefferson and other Southern thinkers believed that the farm and countryside were much better builders of character than large cities. They saw self-employment as the best path to virtue, and the best type of self-employment they believed was farming. Borrowing a page from ancient Roman thinkers, they saw the small freeholder as a strong, disciplined, self-reliant person, the backbone of a free society.

Throughout most of its history, the South has been rural, and most of its economy related to agriculture. Only within the past sixty years or so have most Southerners lived in cities and suburbs. Still the heart of many a Southerner is in the country, the fields, and forests. Hunting and fishing have a greater following in Dixie than in any other region.

To the Southerner even today, the rural life is the free life, unburdened with the cares of the fast-paced urban rat race. Hank Williams Jr. spoke for a wide Southern following when he sang about country folks surviving when city folks can't and the "big hassle" of New York City compared with "the freedom of the rivers and the pines" down South.

Ties to the land keep a Southerner down to earth. Nature has a way of teaching humility. It reinforces the Southerner's Biblical knowledge that you literally reap what you sow. People without these restraints often imagine such vain things as human "liberation" by ignoring God's commandments and nature's laws.

The Southerner is a natural environmentalist, but not, like some environmentalists, a worshiper of nature. Neither does he regard government, like some environmentalists, as the saviour of nature. Laws and regulations will only go so far to guard the natural world. The rest depends on the self-restraint of individuals. In recent times the writings of Wendell Berry of Kentucky have almost become Scripture for all Americans interested in rural life and sustainable agriculture.

With his ties to the land, the Southerner has a sense of place and sentiment about his home. It's part of his identity. An observer pointed out once that Southerners and Northerners differ in the first question they usually ask a person they've just met. The Northerner asks, "What do you do?" The Southerner asks, "Where are you from?" The questions reflect what is important to the questioner.

In the words of Southern writer Margaret Mitchell, the land is what endures. For the Southerner it inspires reverence for the Creator and permanent things. To love the land is to love what is organic and true and to shun the sterile fads of the urban set. It is to revere generations of kin who have lived and died on the same soil.

CHAPTER TWO
THE ASSAULT ON SOUTHERN HERITAGE

SOUTHERN HERITAGE is under heavy attack. It has been so for some time. The force against it is the spirit of a materialist, secular age. The major institutions of this age are Big Government, Big Business, and their propaganda arms of media and education.

The Big Government we have today is the kind of government that Washington, Jefferson, Madison, and other great Southern statesmen and Founders warned us against. It is a jealous god that will have no other gods, or God, before it. This government aggressively seeks to control every aspect of life, while maintaining the outward forms of free government and the Constitution.

Its perversion of the Constitution began with the War for Southern Independence. With the constitutional principle of states' rights in ruins, Northern radicals devised the 14th Amendment to advance federal power. It destroyed the 10th amendment by which the Founders intended to protect state authority from Washington's centralizing power. The 14th Amendment eventually became a blank check for extending Washington's power into local affairs.

The method by which it was enacted showed its sponsors' utter contempt for due process of law and even simple consistency. Throughout the war the North claimed that Southern states had no right to secede and in fact had never left the Union. After the Confederacy's surrender, the defeated Southern states repealed their ordinances of secession and ceased claiming to be outside the Union. Then Northern radicals reversed their position and maintained that the Southern states were not a part of the union and would not be allowed back in until they approved the 14th Amendment! The beaten and ravaged South had no choice but to agree.

In the 20th century, federal courts applied the 14th Amendment with a vengeance against the South often in the name of "civil rights." This rule by unelected judges—unchecked and unbalanced—denied representative government in the Southern states. Many justified it by saying that these steps were necessary to guarantee rights for black citizens. As the abolitionists before them, they never considered or seemed to care that black rights might have been won without destroying the protections of rights for *everyone*.

Using the rhetoric of freedom for blacks, the federal government (often through the courts citing the 14th Amendment) has consistently undercut freedom of association and the right of peoples to maintain their own cultures and communities. Forced busing for "racial balance" in schools was an outstanding example.

Washington and its judicial tyrants have torn communities apart with schemes of busing, with no concern for the wishes of blacks or whites. This social engineering was justified as a way to correct poor education given to blacks. Yet, as the buses rolled on, the quality of education for blacks did not improve. Commonly, it has declined. That is no matter to the tyrants. Education was their pretext; power was their purpose.

Other "civil rights" laws, by courts and Congress, promote more civil wrongs. "Affirmative action" statutes and guidelines have denied companies the freedom to hire persons they deemed the most qualified. These laws were sold as a remedy for discrimination against blacks. Now, for all practical purposes, they require discrimination against whites.

Massive bureaucracy is another legacy of Washington's unbridled reign. Spearheaded by Lyndon Johnson's "Great Society" in the 1960s, layer upon layer of social programs and bureaucracies have burdened productive taxpayers and supported people who would prefer not to work or take responsibility. One consequence has been sharp increases in illegitimate births and family breakdown. The social planners, however, don't seem to mind. More "victims" and social problems mean more jobs and power for them. Particularly hard hit is the black community. As black families and communities have unraveled, the fortunes of their self-appointed saviours have prospered mightily.

Social planners like soft, dependent people who will fit the plans they are told to fit. The softer they become, the more they will need the kind services of the planners. As Big Government grows bigger, the people grow smaller.

America owes a great debt to the many Southern statesmen through American history who have bravely resisted the growth of the Almighty State. Without their influence, it would be far more mighty and menacing than it is today.

* * *

Big Business also began its rise after the War for Southern Independence as corporate monopolies grew in power and influence. Often they relied on the growing government to protect their monopoly power against competition. Conditions for their workers were harsh and oppressive. In many ways slaves in the Old South were treated more humanely. Usually slaves received ample food, shelter, medical treatment, and care in their old age. Northern factory workers often were quite lucky to enjoy any such benefits.

As time passed, rising productivity and the efforts of labour unions secured a better deal for Northern workers. Increasingly the North prospered. The South, well into the 20th century, remained an impoverished economic colony of the North.

Following the war, corrupt carpetbag governments seized control of the Southern States. Through graft, corruption, and ruinous taxation, they plundered what little wealth remained in the former Confederacy. Unlike Washington's generosity toward defeated Germany after World War II, there was no Marshall Plan for Dixie. Northern investors came in and bought up many choice properties at tax foreclosures.

During the 19th and early 20th centuries, railroads were the primary means of trade and transportation. Northern rail companies seriously held back Southern development by charging higher freight rates in the South. This form of discrimination never seemed to bother Northern moralists. Despite all the talk of the "New South," the fact and legacy of Southern poverty still remain.

Yet, in one way, the crippled development of the South was a blessing in disguise because it allowed Southerners for many years to escape the worst of the North's frenzied commercialism.

Big Business, as it has grown from its Northern roots, is also a jealous god and wants no other gods, or God, before it. It wants standardized humans who fit as interchangeable cogs in the production machine. People of distinction and character won't fit so well. And because they aren't inclined to bow down to Mammon, they don't jump quickly when advertising says jump and buy. Such attitudes are a danger to the consumption system and must be discouraged at all costs!

To unreconstructed Southerners and others who would ask "What profits a man if he should lose his soul?" the business interests reply that we in America have "one of the world's highest standards of living." But seldom do the profit sheets of corporatedom show the losses: rising levels of dislocation, drug abuse, alcoholism, divorce, violent crime, environmental degradation, and all the other consequences of a society that knows the price of everything and the value of nothing.

Still the corporations will say that they stand for the virtues and discipline of "free enterprise." It is a strange notion of "free enterprise," indeed, when the government and taxpayers "bail out" corporations that are in trouble from their own misbehaviour. What is really so free about enterprise where the vast majority of men must do as they're told and curry favour with bosses and superiors? Games of "office politics" and "dressing for success" are not likely to produce much independence or character. There was a reason why 19th century Southerners referred disparagingly to employees as "hirelings."

The worst aspect of corporatism is that it tells men that selling their character, independence, and manhood for material "success" is not only acceptable, but is the intelligent, sophisticated, and smart thing to do. Possibly Big Business has brought prosperity, but let us ask once again: What is the price of this prosperity?

It is worth considering too, whether Mammon worship in the long run will even provide riches. The creation of wealth requires inventiveness, initiative, risk-taking, and independent thinking, the very traits that Big Business culture destroys. British writer Somerset Maugham observed that those who seek only wealth will lose their freedom and in the end they will lose their wealth as well.

The true Southerner has nothing against prosperity. He knows well how oppressive poverty can be. He has nothing against making money; he just doesn't believe in making money his God.

The alliance of Big Business and Big Government has two powerful tools to shape people to their thinking. One is mass education; the other is mass media.

Mass education begins with public schooling, or what we should be calling "government schooling." Thanks to decades of federal meddling and educational fads, less and less learning goes on in public schools. High percentages of graduates can barely read, write, do arithmetic, or even think. The Bible, thanks to federal courts, is largely banned from classrooms, and nothing in the way of character instruction goes on.

Students learn little about their country's genuine history and the Constitution. But in "multicultural" studies, they learn that injustice created and built America—and that only the glorious rise of Washington has worked to save us from this frightful heritage!

Public schools promote mass conformity. Standardized instruction promotes standardized people. Vicious peer pressure thrives in this environment and pushes students to do whatever the "in thing" happens to be.

It is not that providing decent education is any deep dark mystery. One-room schoolhouses with only a fraction of the financial resources of schools today did an excellent job of teaching and character building three or four generations ago. Many private schools do now. Basics and discipline are the key. But the interests of centralization don't want parents and society to take and turn this key.

Public schools do not shape the kinds of strong, self-reliant citizens that our Founders saw as necessary for a self-governing society. But these schools are indeed a success in creating the "victims" so beloved by social planners. More than a century ago, Southern theologian Robert Dabney warned that public schools would eventually serve the purposes of an oppressive central state. Who can deny that he was a prophet?

Big Business likes public school products as employees because they are used to fitting into pecking orders without complaint. Lacking spiritual values and culture, many Americans are easy marks, as consumers, for the pitches of corporate advertising. Peer pressure has also taught them the importance of keeping up with the Joneses, and they'll mortgage their souls to do it.

The lack of skills and knowledge among graduates, however, does bother business. It's hard to keep the money machine rolling when so many employees can't read, write, and add. But corporations are figuring to get around the problem by importing trained foreigners to do the work.

University-level education, particularly in such fields as History, English, and so-called "social sciences" is increasingly opposed to traditional American values. On campuses across the country the radical PC (politically correct) movement has declared an all-out war on the Western culture and values that are the foundation of America. Its undisguised aim is to indoctrinate students against God, country, and family. Instead it urges multiculturalism, "thinking globally," and a world without borders.

Many corporations, interestingly enough, like these ideas too, minus the shrill rhetoric. "No borders" means easy movement of plants and capital, and easy access to pools of cheap foreign labour. Though profitable for corporations, these aims do little for American workers or national sovereignty. Two centuries ago Jefferson warned of merchant classes more loyal to their money than their country.

On Southern campuses, PC professors, most from the North, teach Southern students that there is nothing good about their heritage and culture. They indoctrinate these students to believe that their ancestors were wicked and evil men. These professors claim that this type of instruction promotes "tolerance" and "understanding."

A common claim by American educators is that education is the solution to our problems. Modern education, if the truth be told, is the cause of more than a few. For Americans not enrolled in public schools and universities, the powers of centralization and mass society have another shaping device: mass media. Particularly useful for standardizing attitudes and beliefs is television. Newscasters and "public affairs analysts" inform us which ideas are acceptable and which aren't. While this was once limited to "breaking news" and regularly scheduled news programs on local television channels, it is now a 24-hours-a day, 7-days-a-week affair with the domination of cable and satellite news networks. Newscasters, pollsters, specialists, analysts, and other anointed opinion makers continuously dictate to us which ideas are acceptable and which aren't. Southern views are rarely, if ever, acceptable.

To disagree with the High Lords of broadcast is to risk excommunication from the company of "trendy" and "with it" people and be labelled by such names as "racist," "bigot," "extremist," and "redneck." Upscale trendy folk are the first to denounce "hate" and "stereotypes," but also the first to apply them toward traditional Southerners, Christians, and others against whom it is fashionable to be prejudiced.

The print media, or what is left of it, are no less inclined to such slander. Editorial cartoons likening the Confederate battle flag to the banner of Nazi Germany are so common that they have become *cliché*. It would take volumes to catalogue the outrageous slanders heaped upon the South, yet they openly operate in Southern cities all across Dixie with impunity.

Distortion and defamation are common on television "docudramas" and historical pieces dealing with the Old South. "Roots," which portrayed antebellum Southerners as cruel degenerates and fiends, is one which quickly comes to mind. Produced in the late 1970s, it is endlessly re-run on the networks. Another work of this fanciful type is the award-winning "Civil War" series by Ken Burns, which originally aired on PBS. It portrays the Confederacy as a cause of pure evil and is another re-run favourite.

On sitcoms and popular shows a Southern accent is commonly presented as a badge of stupidity—and often one of evil. On crime mysteries if you hear someone speaking Southern, you can guess who-done-it.

But assaults on Southern culture are merely one prong of television's thrust against all culture and decency. Each year sitcoms and other popular entertainment shows compete with each other to explore new depths of vulgarity, violence, and ugliness. The virtues necessary for civilized living: faith, self-control, and sexual restraint, are regularly held up for ridicule.

Woe be to anyone who questions such gutter propaganda! The guardians of Trendydom stand ready to deal out swift revenge. They heap the sort of scorn on critics that they commonly aim at traditional Southerners and other outcasts banished from their grace.

What explains such moral madness? Many trendies in the media and education cheerlead loose sex because they practice what they preach. Just as misery enjoys company, so does guilt. Rationalizations aside, few people can behave like barnyard animals without at least a twinge or two of conscience.

The excitement of degeneracy also helps fill the void left by little or no attachment to faith, family, and community. Most of these trendies are lower-level members of the Establishment. Their missionary work for moral rot serves to fulfil an additional lust felt most keenly by their bosses higher up in the Establishment—the lust for power. Just as it is easy to control ignorant and fearful people, so too it is relatively easy to corral herds of folks with scarcely a notion of self-control, self-respect, and virtue.

Equally vulgar and destructive as television programming are the commercials that instruct us to believe that we can buy or borrow our way to happiness. Far be it that we should question the Unholy Grail of greed and keeping up with the Joneses. If we did, the companies sponsoring the ads might lose some dollars. It's too bad that this advertising has to assault our senses and manipulate us, but that is the price of "progress" as some call it.

In short, television and other mass media assist the erosion of character and personhood that modern government, business, and education promote. The media work to bring men down to the lowest common level of morals, values, and knowledge. Such is the only state where men can truly be made equal. It is a condition beloved by the social planners because such equal men are perfectly interchangeable parts for social plans.

CHAPTER THREE

HOW TO DEFEND SOUTHERN HERITAGE

T HE POWER OF the corporate-statist powers (henceforth referred to as "the Establishment") is indeed formidable, but just as in the days of Elijah, there is still a remnant that refuses to bend a knee to Baal. And foremost in the ranks of the American remnant are traditional Southerners.

Sustaining these Southerners is a memory and heritage of heroism against great odds. Old—and better—times are not completely forgotten in Dixie.

Yet to stand and prevail against the modern powers of darkness will require more than memory. A people who live in the past will die there, too. To prevail and live, they must adapt past values to present conditions. This will require creativity, invention, and work.

These traits are a part of Southern heritage as shown during the South's war for independence. Within a few short months, Southerners created the machinery of a new nation, and the necessities of war production became the mother of many inventions. Southerners then adapted well to the demands of their times, and only a mystery of fate denied them victory.

Yet many today who admire that generation will not act as it acted. They simply want to bask in the reflection of their ancestors' glory. They endlessly recall the details of past battles, while ignoring the battles of their own day. That does no honour to those ancestors and leaves no future for their descendants.

HERITAGE DEFENSE ON A PERSONAL LEVEL

For the Southerner who would struggle today so that his culture will have a tomorrow, a question commonly comes up: "Just what can one person do?" The answer is that it depends on the person.

Modern society aims to destroy courage, determination, and self-reliance. But an individual who stands up to this attack and overcomes it is someone who can accomplish a great deal.

Overcoming does not come by accident, but by development of body, mind, and spirit. All require activity. One useful first step is walking over to the television and turning it off. As we have seen, most modern programming pollutes the mind and soul, and sitting for hours before the tube does little for the body. After turning off the television keep on walking—maybe around the block. Do that for a few days, and then run. Depending on your age, take up a sport or hobby that demands a little exertion. Digging a garden can be useful—and it will provide some good fresh food.

Learn and practice nutrition. Poor food causes more disease and psychological problems than many people realize. Modern food production is often more geared to corporate profits than to the well-being of consumers. When possible, eat food as God made it, the less processing the better.

A healthy body promotes a healthy mind. Yet just as the body needs its own kind of exercise, so does the mind. That exercise is the quest for knowledge. Each step of understanding leads to greater insight and awareness. A person with knowledge is one who can see clearly to lead others.

To stand effectively for Southern tradition requires thorough knowledge of that tradition. A good place to start is speaking with older members of your family about what they remember of times past. Book knowledge is important, too. Two excellent books to read and meditate upon are Richard Weaver's *The Southern Tradition at Bay* and *I'll Take My Stand* by the 12 Southern Agrarians. Two other good books are Michael Grissom's *Southern by the Grace of God* and *The Last Rebel Yell*. The websites of the Society of Independent Southern Historians and the Abbeville Institute contain a treasury of quality material on Southern life and history.

Knowledge, however, is ultimately a vain thing without inspiration and values. For the traditional Southerner, the source of these is the Christian religion and the heritage of Western culture.

But a word of caution is necessary here, because the faith taught from many Southern pulpits today is scarcely the noble faith of Lee and Jackson. It is a weak creed which teaches men to be fearful and unmanly—doormats on which evil can wipe its feet. Sadly, it is no coincidence that these are the very traits that the worldly establishment of government and business promote. A majority of Southern churches have yielded to the spirit of the world for the sake of lucre and conformist "respectability."

Also these churches teach the modern cult of "equalitarianism" rather than the order, rank, and distinctions affirmed by the Bible. This cult makes God the "buddy" of man, instead of his Father and Lord. It tries to erase all boundaries of tribe and nation. Supposedly this rebuilding of the Tower of Babel will promote "brotherhood" and tolerance.

Once again, people without real identity and culture make good cogs and building blocks for corporations and planners. As would-be rulers have long recognized, false religious prophets are good for profits and power.

For the sake of his soul, the Southerner today who would be true to God—and the faith of his fathers—must walk lonesome valleys and rediscover ancient truths. Admittedly, this will not be an easy task. But this narrow path, as Christ forewarned, is the only sure route to salvation.

DEFENSE OF HERITAGE OF THE FAMILY/COMMUNITY LEVEL

Individual effort, however, is only the first step toward a renewal of Southern culture. No man is an island, and man finds his strength and fulfilment through association with his fellow men. Many conservative Southerners have fallen victim to the Yankee notion of "rugged individualism" which in practice means self-advancement with little regard for others. The Southern virtue is individuality, the flowering of unique personalities and talents. This flower grows best from the fertile soil of blood ties, friendship, and community.

The deepest and most important tie, as we have seen, is family. And it is against the family that the powers-that-be have levelled their mightiest artillery. They have sold society the lie that personal advancement and money are more important than love, loyalty, and kin. Among the casualties are broken homes and broken men, women, and children.

It is wrong to believe that politicians talking about "family values" can solve the problem. They, in fact, have caused much of it. The only effective resistance must come from a change of heart and mind. People must simply decide to put family first, regardless of the costs. Southerners, with their historic sense of kinship, should properly lead the way.

Doing it will require creativity to circumvent and outwit the powers and principalities now pulling the family apart. Today mothers, fathers, and children often live in separate worlds. One simple step to bring such strangers together is the simple decision that everyone will gather around the table each evening for supper. No television should be on to distract attention and conversation. It should go without saying that sending or receiving phone calls and text messages or checking out social media on one's smartphone or tablet is unacceptable behaviour at the dinner table and for the same reason.

Most important are tasks where everyone participates and works together for the common good. Family gardening is a good example. For many city and suburb-dwelling Southerners, it can be a way—even if to a limited degree—to regain closeness to the soil and the cycles of nature. For children the garden teaches responsibility and the lesson that you literally reap what you sow. For the adults raising some food it is a step, even if a small one, toward greater independence and self-reliance.

One thing certainly to be said for family gardening is that it helps the family budget. It provides food cheaper than the supermarket. And if the crops are organically grown and not saturated with pesticides, they will maintain health much better than the produce from large-scale farming and factory processing.

Another important point is that the day will come when home-grown food will become more a necessity than a hobby. The secret to America's abundance of food has been adequate numbers of family farms, especially where family members have had close personal involvement in production. On such farms much hard work is done as a labour of love and not for immediate profit. The Southerner Wendell Berry has become the world's spokesman for sustainable agriculture and family farming. (See *What Are People For?*)

But the trend of farming for some time has been toward fewer farms and larger farms. The larger farms, even if family owned, function increasingly like corporations. This being the case, workers must be hired to do work once done for love and pride of ownership, and the extra expense could push up food prices. The tendency of a few large farms being monopolistic raises the prospect of more expensive food. If these developments come about, the home gardener could avoid, to some extent, food prices far higher than what we're used to now.

People who don't want to become involved in full-time gardening might consider helping to support a farm family. Several city families could contract with a farmer to provide them food. Store-bought food may be cheaper, but the farmer could offer fresh organic produce. From time to time, the city parents and their children could go to the farm and help with the harvest. They could enjoy working together while getting a taste of country life.

Another way to strengthen family unity, though it admittedly is not for everyone, is a family business. The corporate economics of modern America pull families apart. Fathers go to jobs, and mothers, often for need or personal fulfilment, take jobs outside the home. The children have little real idea what their parents do and, as a consequence, have little in common to share with them. What the typical family gains in income today is often matched in the weakening of family ties.

A family business meets this problem. The family earns income by practicing teamwork. Husbands and wives pull together, as they work on common tasks. Home businesses avoid the problem of women having to choose between career and homemaking. They can do both with a different emphasis at different times of their lives. Children are a part of the team, and under their parents' leadership, they learn real life skills and responsibilities. All have an incentive to labour hard because they are working for themselves, and one another, rather than a boss. In business for themselves, they learn independence as well as cooperation.

The business need not be a full-time operation. Even a side-line operation can be helpful for strengthening family ties and generating extra income. Family gardens and family businesses are but two ideas for activities to unify the immediate family. Another is home schooling. Today this is a growing movement throughout the country, as parents tire of public schools which undermine parental authority, and promote fads of "values clarification" and sex education at the expense of reading, writing, and math.

According to some estimates, more than one and a half million pupils today are now receiving instruction, at some level, from their parents. Home schooling offers many advantages. The instructing parent can tailor lessons to the child's level of ability and attention span. For this reason, the school day can be shorter. It takes less time to teach one child than to spread teaching out over a class of thirty. Home schooling is no new invention. It was common in the Old South and other parts of the country during the 18th and 19th centuries. Home schooling helped to produce literate and cultured men and women.

Today, of course, the "experts" will tell us that parents generally aren't qualified to provide the type of knowledge necessary to run an advanced technical society. And admittedly it may be that advanced math and science require teachers with training in those areas. But elementary schooling, during the most formative years of life, requires little more than reading, writing, and arithmetic—the very skills that public schools increasingly seem unable to teach.

Contrary to claims of the professional "educators," if parents can read, write, and do arithmetic, they can teach their children to do them, too. The educators, like so many modern "experts," want people to doubt their abilities so that they will do as the "experts" bid and pay for the privilege. With the growth of home schooling, many materials and teaching guides are available to assist parent-teachers. Home-schooled students are invariably proving themselves better educated than the graduates of government schools.

For Southern parents, home schooling offers the opportunity to teach Southern values and history. They can also pass on their religious faith. They need not worry about school bureaucrats force-feeding their children anti-Christian and multi-cultural propaganda.

The immediate family, however, should not be the only interest or concern. Just as important is building up the extended family.

Cousins need to know cousins, nephews their uncles, and grandparents their grandchildren. Building these networks of blood and kin will re-create a likeness of the clans of Old Scotland. Relatives can pitch in to help one another with support such as job contacts and various types of professional advice. A stockbroker may help the others with financial advice, or a carpenter may help with building houses. Members of these clans also could help others by providing jobs in their businesses.

As time goes on and the bonds of these extended families grow, they might organize formally. Perhaps they might elect ruling elders. Among other functions, these elders could help settle disputes among clan members. In many cases, such voluntary handling of disputes would save everyone the cost of an increasingly expensive legal system, where lawyers grow fat at the expense of everyone else. Other elders of the community, particularly those who have run successful businesses, might take on the task of providing advice to young businessmen and entrepreneurs.

If difficult political and economic times lie ahead, these ties that bind will offer much security. Isolated individuals are much at the mercy of big institutions and bureaucracies. Clans and kinfolks pulling together are a strong arm of defense.

Family reunions are one way of bringing the extended family together. Southerners hold quite a few of these already. A way to help make reunions a regular and sure thing is for families to pool their money and purchase a vacation cabin where single families can go for vacation and where all can come together for reunions. At the reunions, family members can sing old Southern songs, square dance, share family lore, and just plain relax. It can be a time to discuss plans, dreams, and ideas. Particular items might be business ventures or political projects.

As clans grow stronger they should reach out and make connections with other Southern-minded clans and individuals. Southern heritage and historical societies are good places to make contacts. Two leading examples are the Sons of Confederate Veterans (SCV), an organization of male descendants of Confederate soldiers and the United Daughters of the Confederacy (UDC), a society of female descendants.

A network of families, clans, and associations is the first of two steps to a revitalized Southern community and culture. The next step is for that network to take initiative to influence society in ways congenial to Southern values. (Political action will be considered in Chapter 5.) This initiative, small-scale at first, should begin locally.

An example might be a committee of writers to reply publicly to anti-Southern disparagements in the media. This could be an informal group of family and friends, or a committee within the SCV or some other organization. Another step could be asking a local mayor to issue an official proclamation for Confederate Memorial Day. Of course, all genuine Southerners in the community should organize and participate in ceremonies for that occasion.

As ties grow stronger in the revived Southern community, members could set their sights on long-range enterprises and projects. Unrelated individuals, following the lead of families, might form small businesses. The rest of the community, in turn, would patronize those businesses, or perhaps pool capital for business loans. To return these favours, the businesses could help provide funding for community efforts.

A local-level project might be a private school stressing

traditional Southern values. Home schooling is not possible for everyone. A private school could provide good teaching, as well as an escape hatch from public schooling. Another project might be religious meetings in homes, like those of the early Church, where Southerners could enjoy Christian fellowship and refine their faith and values.

In time, members of the Southern community might decide to move into the same neighbourhood, or perhaps move to the country to create a small settlement. This closeness would make it easier for individual members and families to work together on schooling, business, church work, and other activities.

By coming together, either in physical or spiritual closeness, the community could deploy its new-found unity against social problems. One is crime. Southerners bound together by living heritage might organize neighbourhood watch committees, or if conditions demanded it, they might organize foot and car patrols in conjunction with police. This would be in the finest tradition of Southern manhood and chivalry in defense of the weak and helpless members of society. From these same motives, Southerners might move to attack pornography and the vile threat it poses to family values.

With local tasks underway, the Southern community might next consider regional objectives. Of crucial importance, in the long run, is higher education. Southerners must wage a war of ideas and regain at least some influence on Southern campuses. It is there, as we have seen, where the ideas that shape society are formed. The task will not be easy, but it must be undertaken. One useful step would be for the small number of pro-Southern scholars still in the colleges and universities to organize and coordinate their activities.

Another one on the part of alumni is to put pressure, particularly the financial pressure of withholding contributions, on schools that refuse to permit pro-Southern views. The Abbeville Institute has done great work in providing students with knowledge unavailable in our present centers of "learning."

In addition, a long-range high-priority task is founding a "Southern University" where Southern scholars can set the direction of Southern values and culture without interference from hostile alien influences. There the sons and daughters of the South can grow in learning and appreciation of their heritage.

A regional media will be necessary to promote Southern values among the masses. There was a time when the acquisition of a newspaper or gaining access to radio or television outlets was the only options available. All that has changed. The Internet has opened up a world of opportunities for producing and distributing Southern-friendly publications, podcast and/or live audio feeds, as well as video productions. These new venues of mass communication do not require a lot of technical expertise, are comparatively inexpensive, and can be marketed to a much wider audience. The Southern community as a whole should make a point to patronize Southern media and their advertisers regardless of the methods employed to reach the Southern people.

The church and religion are crucial too. As Southerners gain deeper understanding of their Southern Christian roots, they will realize all the more the need for deeper spiritual nourishment than the offerings of the New South's McDonaldized fast faith churches. In time, the spirituality kindled in Southern homes and local communities may grow into a South-wide movement. A community which endures must have a spiritual center.

A revitalized Southern culture would have a great influence throughout the country. It could inspire other American communities to look to their roots to find beneficial direction for the present and future.

CHAPTER FOUR

THE ESTABLISHMENT WILL RESIST

SOUTHERN REVIVAL

O F COURSE, THE POWERS of centralization are not going to sit idly by while these efforts proceed in the South. They will bitterly resist "ordinary" people taking charge of their lives, and they will use political action and law to do it.

To weaken family ties, the Establishment hopes to maintain and increase the taxes which particularly burden productive families. A more direct attack on the family, now growing as a movement, is the legal right of bureaucrats to intrude into family life under the pretext of "child abuse." Sometimes "child abuse" is defined as the biblically-mandated discipline of spanking.

Many believe that the end result of this "child abuse" crusade will be State control of children. Parents would have authority over their own children only to the extent allowed by government.

In education, the potentates of public schooling will not yield their monopolies without a fight. The Establishment as a whole has an enormous stake in keeping its grip on the minds of young people.

Private schooling and home schooling will come under increasing attack.

Sometimes the attack will be subtle. Today, with disgust toward public schooling at perhaps an all-time high, much is heard of the idea of school vouchers, which would give tax money to parents who wish to send their children to private schools. Even some of the establishment media seem friendly to the idea. The catch is that wherever government money goes, government control goes also.

As long as private schooling and home schooling exist, the Establishment will have to suffer the embarrassment of its public schools being outperformed. This they cannot allow to continue. If subtle approaches don't work, then not so subtle ones will follow. They already have in some places, such as those states which have tried to outlaw or greatly restrict home schooling.

As for crime and community defense, the Establishment legal system will continue its long-standing effort to put the rights of criminals above those of law-abiding citizens. When citizens take steps to defend themselves, they can count on the media to wail about "vigilantes" and people who take the law into their own hands. The Establishment, actually, isn't too worried about crime. Its well-to-do members can usually buy their way into neighbourhoods where it is not a great problem.

A key point to consider is that crime can be useful to those who want to centralize power. People demoralized by fear of lawbreakers will be timid, and not too zealous to stand up for their rights. Also, such a people will beg for more laws and police in hope of security. Big Government is more than happy to provide them, even to the point of a police state.

Effective self-defense and community defense require the right to keep and bear arms. The Founding Fathers, as we have seen, recognized this basic right of a free people in the Second Amendment to the Constitution. But as free-thinking people are not to the liking of the Establishment, its media will keep on beating the drums for gun control.

As for combating pornography and other types of vulgarity, the legal system will pose many roadblocks. Supposedly it violates "freedom of expression" to regulate and control smut. Interestingly, for almost the first two hundred years of the nation's life, no one made a connection between the constitutional guarantee of free speech and material which can only appeal to the lowest instincts.

In business, big corporations will fight to keep their power and semi-monopoly status. They don't want small companies springing up to give them competition. Because of innumerable laws supposedly for the public interest, small businesses must contend with heavy loads of regulations and paperwork. For the big companies these are not so burdensome because they can afford large staffs to handle the maze of regulations created by the modern bureaucratic state. They have no interest in seeing such regulation removed. Often they favour it.

This is unfortunate for society because small business provides most of the country's new jobs, and it is also the source of newest inventions. Small enterprises are more inventive because individual initiative is not stifled by bureaucracy, "office politics," and conformist thinking.

Of all the Establishment's legal/political threats probably the greatest legal threat to the South—and all America—is the current open door to immigration which is allowing unprecedented numbers and varieties of foreigners into the United States. Coupled with this policy is Washington's steadfast refusal to take any effective steps to stem record levels of illegal immigration.

Out-of-control immigration has something to offer every player on the Establishment team. For business, there is cheap labour; for "internationalists," a means to destroy national identity; for welfare bureaucracies, new pools of impoverished "victims;" for centralizers of political power, the anarchy of diverse peoples and tongues as a ready-made excuse for more government to maintain order.

The internationalists constantly harp on the need for multiculturalism, even as they strive to uproot Southern culture. Political attacks on the symbols of the Old South are part of this effort of "cultural cleansing." New South politicians who commit acts of suppression of Confederate symbols are hailed as national heroes. Self-seekers and often social climbers, they strive to ingratiate themselves with their Establishment "betters" in the North.

The Establishment is supremely confident that its political, legal, and economic power can erase Southern heritage and prevent its revival. For half a century, "experts" have been predicting and applauding the demise of the South as a distinctive region, but it has not happened yet.

Such forecasts should not trouble true Southerners unduly. It is a common ploy of colonialists and their native sycophants to predict the end of subject peoples and cultures in the name of "progress." The British Empire boasted that the Irishness of Ireland would fade away and the Soviet commissars said the same of their captive nationalities.

Those empires are gone, but the peoples they ruled are still peoples. Quite often, particularly in the long-run, the ties of memory and blood are stronger than pomp, power, and laws.

CHAPTER FIVE

Steps to Maintain and Defend Southern Revival

T O MEET THE ESTABLISHMENT'S legal/political attack, the Southern community will have no choice but to enter the political field. It must begin at the local level, learn the political ropes, and then advance to the state and federal levels. Always, however, it must stress the Southern principles that government decision-making should be as close as possible to the people, and as limited as possible. A general rule should always be: keep the federal government out of what should properly be state affairs, and the state out of what should properly be local affairs.

The following are general proposals for a Southern legislative agenda:

Agriculture

1) Provide tax breaks for small-scale family farms. Also require that such farms be assessed for tax purposes on their current use value as farms, rather than potential suburban and commercial use. This will help prevent

speculators from driving farmers off the land and help keep productive farmland from being paved over and developed.

2) Require agricultural programs at state universities to gear more research and advice to small-scale agriculture.

3) End subsidies to Big Agriculture.

BUSINESS

1) Revise the tax structure to encourage small business. Specifically, work to keep taxes on small business low and to remove regulations requiring unnecessary paperwork.

2) End subsidies to large corporations.

3) Encourage Southern rather than absentee ownership of land and business.

CIVIL RIGHTS

1) Establish a firm legal distinction between public and private activity. In public activities (defined primarily by the expenditure of tax money), governments would enforce access to all qualified taxpaying citizens. This would apply to such areas as voting, public employment, and government-funded education, including the university level. With education and employment, merit rather than quotas would be the standard for selection. In private activity (that involving no government money or government contacts), anti-discrimination statutes would not apply. Examples are private schools and clubs.

2) An end to social engineering by unelected judges.

CULTURE

1) Defend the right of states, localities and individuals to display the Confederate flag in public places.

2) Enact local, state, and national preservation laws to protect historic homes, buildings, monuments, and sites.

EDUCATION

1) Remove restrictions on home schooling where they exist and maintain the right to home schooling where it is established.

2) Exempt parents from public school taxes who do home schooling or send their children to private schools.

3) Increase oversight of public schools by parents who have children in them.

ENVIRONMENT

1) As much as possible, make the violation of rights and property, rather than bureaucratic planning, the basis of environmental law. To illustrate, government would impose fewer direct environmental controls, but individuals and institutions would have more encouragement to sue for damages for provable loss to their health and property from pollution.

2) Enact tax laws to penalize polluters, and give tax breaks to companies to take steps to reduce pollution.

FAMILY LIFE

1) Repeal tax laws which put a greater weight on married couples with children than singles.

2) Repeal no-fault divorce laws which facilitate the break-up of marriages.

3) Resist laws which would ignore valid differences between men and women.

4) Resist special privileges for the Gay, Bisexual, Lesbian, Transgender (GBLT) "community."

5) Resist abortion on demand.

6) Repeal welfare laws which encourage single mothers and families on public assistance to have children, at the expense of taxpaying families.

7) Repeal laws which, under the pretext of fighting child abuse, give bureaucrats the right to step into private family matters.

GOVERNMENT

1) Defend the rights of the states against federal control and work to expand those rights in keeping with the 10th amendment of the Constitution.

IMMIGRATION

1) Reduce the current level of immigration so that numbers and diversity do not overwhelm natural resources, national character, and domestic tranquility.

2) Take effective steps to halt illegal immigration, including the emergency stationing of troops on the border, empowerment of local law enforcement to enforce immigration laws, and a cutoff of all tax-paid benefits and privileges for illegal aliens.

Law & Criminal Justice

1) Rewrite the criminal codes to stress the rights of law-abiding society above the rights of criminals.

2) Shorten the time between apprehension of criminals and punishment.

3) Crack down on violent criminals. Create a policy of letting non-violent offenders do community work outside of prison to pay off their debt to society. Wages they earn would pay losses to victims of their crimes.

4) Uphold and affirm the death penalty for the capital crime of premeditated murder.

CHAPTER SIX

INVENTION & INNOVATION

THE FUTURE FRONTIERS FOR SOUTHERN RENEWAL

COMMUNITY BUILDING and the legislative agenda will do much to revive Southern spirit and identity. Yet by themselves they will not be able to deal a decisive blow to the Establishment because it will still control most of the commanding heights of wealth and power. To storm, or at least neutralize, these heights, Southern families, clans, and communities will need a new vision of political and economic liberty to go on the offensive. The past is where to look for such a vision.

The people of the Old South were generally self-sufficient in their communities. Whether on large plantations or small farms, they did not need, with a few exceptions, goods and services from the outside. They grew most of their own food, spun many of their own clothes, and often sawed their own lumber to build houses. The South had few large cities in antebellum times because it had little need for them as hubs of commerce. The North saw this as a sign of Southern "backwardness."

Northerners then, particularly in the Northeast, were modernizing with factories, specialization of labour, and new technology. The South, in its turn, condemned this modernization which exalted material values above all others, crowded people together, and led men to trade independence for an uncertain pay check. This system, however, did generate wealth and national power. And that industrial power is what defeated the South.

Today, the South is part of the system of centralization. The question Southerners must ask is how the South can get out of it, or at least far enough out of it to preserve its historic identity. Stronger families and renewed communities are important steps, but, once again, they are at heavy disadvantage against the modern economy.

Due to its pressures, most people have to work for others, and commonly they have to move from place to place to find employment. This constant uprooting of people makes it difficult for them to forge ties of family and friendship. It also weakens the Southerner's sense of place, his ties to the land, and a particular identity.

One step, already mentioned, to combat this need for movement is for families and Southern communities to create their own businesses. This was once a drawback for rural communities because of their proximity to the cities. This is no longer the case. With advances in technology, one can conduct business anywhere in the world with anyone in the world. A good idea or product can be marketed and sold with a computer and Internet access. People in any small Southern town have access to the same information and tools as people operating in the big cities.

The solution lies in creating communities and economies that can, for the most part, stand by themselves. New technology is the key. Some traditional Southerners, however, may shy away from it.

They associate technology with so called "progress," "bigness," and the "Modern World." This misgiving is understandable, but not accurate. Technology is no better or worse than the values of the people who create or use it.

The apostles of bigness use technology to corral and control men, but free men can use it to promote freedom. The four years of the Southern Confederacy illustrate this point. At the beginning of the war, a South with few industries faced the nearly overwhelming task of equipping its war machine. But necessity proved to be the mother of Southern invention, and Southerners met technical challenges with amazing ingenuity.

As the Establishment wages its fight against the South, Southern ingenuity may again have to rise to the occasion. Advances in technology have opened opportunities heretofore unknown. It has certainly made it easier for governments and bureaucracies to keep tabs on us. But as many are finding today, it can be a most useful tool in promoting personal freedom.

With the Internet, one can share ideas with others. In a significant way, it allows an individual to bypass the censorship of the mass media. Computers can also be used for online publishing of news and opinion—another way of bypassing mass media control.

But more importantly, in line with community-building, technology is offering some people the ability to telecommute, that is, to stay at home and work regardless of the location of the office of their employer. The only limit is the ability to access the Internet. Even if cable or DSL Internet access is unavailable, satellite access is practically universal. Some fields where this kind of working arrangement already exists are writing, data processing, accounting, and various types of consulting. As time goes on, many other fields will adapt their business model to take advantage of this technological reality; many already have. For more independent and ambitious people, working online opens a wide range of possibilities for self-employment.

It is possible for some people to beat the system by the methods mentioned above. Admittedly, still, it is a hard system to get around. In so many ways, the Establishment's technology and its economics are powerful currents pushing us toward centralization. Energy is a prime example. To obtain the power we need for production and comfort, we must submit to centralized systems requiring huge investments. Thus it is hard to escape at least some control by big utilities and oil, gas, and coal companies.

Great power—literally and figuratively—is in few hands. This power quite often influences governments, and almost everyone must bend to it, if for no other reason than having to pay utility and fuel bills.

Possible solutions are new energy sources, particularly ones adapted to small-scale use. Solar power is a possibility. No one can monopolize the sun. Some "experts" (perhaps in the pay of the energy companies) claim that solar power can never really meet our needs. But progress with solar technology suggests that it might someday, at least where the sun shines adequately. Ideally it will offer equipment that individuals can adapt for their personal uses.

Other possibilities are new technologies which would allow individuals, families and small communities to tap energy sources common to a locality, such as wind and streams. (Two books which effectively argue the case for small-scale community economies are E.F. Schumacher's *Small is Beautiful* and *Human Scale* by Kirkpatrick Sale.)

Perhaps the greatest obstacle to economic independence is the overspecialization of the modern corporate economy. If you want clothes or shoes to wear, you usually have to buy them from a chain store or their equivalent on the Internet. But would it be possible for local small-scale industries, or home industries, to manufacture them and other needed products? The standard argument against such a proposal is that mass-produced factory production is always cheaper. Or is it?

One who disagreed was Ralph Borsodi, a social thinker who wrote during the 1930s. (Two books explaining his ideas are *This Ugly Civilization* and *Flight from the City*.) Borsodi believed that cottage industries, with adoptions of the technology existing at that time, could provide many goods as cheap or more cheaply than mass production. Taking the example of canned foods, he demonstrated that canning at home made more economic sense than mass-production canning. Borsodi maintained that the advantages large corporations have in competition often are the result of the law being stacked in their favour.

The independence provided by home- or community-based industries was equally important to Borsodi. He stressed that when people are in charge of their lives, and not the economic pawns of bosses and corporate boards, they develop strength of character. Like Jefferson, he saw that it was difficult for men to act as free men with the threat of unemployment hanging over their heads.

Some might object that individuals, particularly the young,

might find these communities too confining and would want to leave. In keeping with the Southern belief of liberty, they should have every right to go. Still, many would appreciate the knowledge that if they lose their jobs in the outside world they would always have a haven of family or community employment to return to. This "safety net" would make them more confident as workers and citizens than most of their "outside" co-workers.

Another strong argument Borsodi used for self-sufficient communities was the pleasure of craftsmanship people experience when they design and make many of the goods they use. When one generation passes on crafts and skills to another, ties between parents and children grow stronger. In a homestead or community economy, men and women could find the flexibility to live and work in ways in keeping with their innate and different natures. The existing economy causes untold misery by forcing a unisex role on the sexes. Nothing could be farther from the traditional Southern ideals of manhood and womanhood.

Still another benefit of generally self-sufficient homesteads and communities is that they permit variety in work. Schedules could be much more flexible than with a standard-wage job. A person could do "brain work" in the morning and manual labour in the afternoon. The health of mind and body require a variety of work; the employee/wage system commonly offers soul-killing repetition.

Borsodi denounced the centralized industrial system for using technology to enslave men rather than free them. Making men fit machines and rat-race time schedules, he affirmed, is destructive of human personality. Many of Borsodi's criticisms were quite similar to those of the Southern Agrarians (*I'll Take My Stand*) who also wrote during the 1930s.

Sadly, their warnings and Borsodi's went unheeded. The centralized corporate system produced such wealth that few people noticed the spiritual costs. More might have cared if they had realized that these costs necessarily would translate into real and tangible losses. With depleted spirits sapping the will of Americans to produce and excel, the money-making machine is running down. Debt-fueled consumption provides an illusion of prosperity, while "American" corporations, more concerned with quick cash than country, are shipping their operations abroad to take advantage of cheap labour and lax environmental laws. Despite assurances from politicians, the American economy is in trouble. Our great middle class, the mainstay of our national greatness, is slowly but surely dwindling.

Unleashing the energy and inventiveness of the Southern community, and other communities, might be a way to reverse our economic decline. If we love our neighbours and our work more than we love money, we'll end up with better neighbours, and probably more prosperity as well.

Advanced solar power systems, and small-scale manufacturing plants will take some time to develop. But other advances could be within relatively easy reach.

One might be finding ways to use energy more efficiently; that is, more power for a dollar. This could reduce dependence on large corporations. That, of course, would reduce their profits, something they might not take lying down. Around many mechanics' shops, stories circulate about "good ol' boys" who have invented carburetors that can get 100 miles to a gallon. (Contrary to Yankee stereotypes about stupid Southern "rednecks," quite a few of our "good ol' boys" have a first-rate mechanical knack.) But strangely, the stories go, these inventors cannot get patents. Some stories tell of inventors being threatened with physical harm.

The Southern community could provide two remedies. A patent might be recognized within the community and royalties paid to the inventor by its members. If necessary, the community could defend the inventor. It might also promote invention by providing loans to inventors.

Some of these ideas may now sound impractical. But with the corporate system failing the nation in so many ways, it is plain that Southerners and all Americans will have to try new economic directions if we want to maintain a decent standard of living. Small-scale, family-managed businesses have a proven track record among the Chinese people of Taiwan, Hong Kong, and Singapore. These were the engines which raised those lands from poverty to prosperity. There is no reason why the same idea can't work for us.

The success of those Asian lands, which are largely urban, refutes the argument that Southern principles would have little to offer American urban areas where, like it or not, most people will continue to live. True enough, urban centers are not the most congenial places for Southerners, but Southern values can make them more congenial.

A problem in many American big cities is lack of community and small-scale enterprise. The values of the South could make real contributions to solving these problems. They also could inspire efforts to bring the country to the city. One example is community gardening. In many of our big cities there are wide stretches of vacant lots and abandoned properties. Gardening could begin here. It would bring people together, and could also provide welfare recipients a chance to keep their self-respect by doing useful work and learning a skill of self-sufficiency. Other possibilities are tree planting and more parks to make cities more livable. Southern living has appeal and offers hope to all Southerners, black and white.

Along with meeting urban needs, a revival of Southern values could aid the environment. The traditional Southern love of the land is a sentiment well-adapted to promoting conservation stewardship. Development of efficient small-scale technology would be most helpful to a world having to cope with pollution and depletion of resources. Sooner or later these problems will force changes in our way of life. It would be better to deal with them at our leisure in advance, rather than being forced to make them in haste under the threat of some environmental catastrophe or threatened loss of resources.

To be sure—whether in big cities or traditional Southern settings—not everybody will have the talents necessary to pioneer small-scale enterprise, and it's probably just as well that they don't. We need some large-scale manufacturing to keep some of the better features of our society. Such goods as automobiles and military equipment for national security immediately come to mind.

Even so, a small number of pioneers seeking and finding new and better ways of living, to whatever extent their particular talents enable them, would have effects far beyond their numbers. Like the relatively tiny rudder that turns a big ship, they could steer society in a new direction.

The time is ripe to set a new course of living and making a living. Southerners and other Americans must understand that to depend on the Establishment is to participate in our own destruction. If we are to be saved, we must save ourselves by striking out on our own, a person at a time, a family at a time, and a community at a time, to build a future worth living as free men and women.

Conclusion

BE WARNED THAT THE ROUTE to Southern renewal will offer hardship, toil, and difficulty. It will require blazing new trails while following ancient directions. It is not a mission for weaklings.

Still it is one that Southerners may undertake with the absolute knowledge that their cause is right and just. The Establishment claims to advance human rights, compassion, and "progress." Yet behind the rhetoric the truth is showing ever more plainly—the reality of power-elitists who seek to reduce their fellow men to the level of cattle in order to rule them.

Threats to liberty and decency far less than this once called Southerners to sacrifice and heroism. They knew their heritage and their God. The Establishment despises both. With these stark alternatives now before them, modern Southerners must now heed the command of Israel's ancient prophet: Decide ye today whom ye will serve.

ABOUT THE AUTHOR

JOHN VINSON, a native of Athens, Georgia, has been the president of the American Immigration Control Foundation since 1990 and was editor for *Americans for Immigration Control* from 1996 to 2003. Vinson is a graduate of Duke University (MA, History) and the University of Georgia (MA, Historic Preservation). His career includes working at the *Savannah Morning News* as an editorial writer; editorial page editor for the *Colorado Springs Gazette-Telegraph*; and as a writer for the *Georgia Soil and Water Conservation Commission* and the *Small Business Development Center*, both in Athens, Georgia.

Mr. Vinson resides with his wife in Monterey, Virginia. They have one child.

AVAILABLE FROM SHOTWELL PUBLISHING

IF YOU ENJOYED THIS BOOK, perhaps some of our other titles will pique your interest. The following titles are currently available from Shotwell at Amazon and all major online book retailers.

A Legion of Devils: Sherman in South Carolina by Karen Stokes

Annals of the Stupid Party: Republicans Before Trump by Clyde N. Wilson

Carolina Love Letters by Karen Stokes

Confederaphobia: An American Epidemic by Paul C. Graham

Dismantling the Republic by Jerry C. Brewer

Dixie Rising: Rules for Rebels by James R. Kennedy

Emancipation Hell: The Tragedy Wrought By Lincoln's Emancipation Proclamation by Kirkpatrick Sale

Lies My Teacher Told Me: The True History of the War for Southern Independence by Clyde N. Wilson

Maryland, My Maryland: The Cultural Cleansing of a Small Southern State by Joyce Bennett.

Nullification: Reclaiming Consent of the Governed by Clyde N. Wilson

Punished with Poverty: The Suffering South by James R. & Walter D. Kennedy

Segregation: Federal Policy or Racism? by John Chodes

Southern Independence. Why War?- The War to Prevent Southern Independence by Dr. Charles T. Pace

Southerner, Take Your Stand! by John Vinson

Washington's KKK: The Union League During Southern Reconstruction by John Chodes.

When the Yankees Come: Former South Carolina Slaves Remember Sherman's Invasion. Edited with Introduction by Paul C. Graham

The Yankee Problem: An American Dilemma by Clyde N. Wilson

FREE BOOK OFFER

Sign-up for new release notification and receive a FREE DOWNLOADABLE EDITION of *Lies My Teacher Told Me: The True History of the War for Southern Independence* by Dr. Clyde N. Wilson by visiting FreeLiesBook.com or by texting the word "Dixie" to 345345. You can always unsubscribe and keep the book, so you've got nothing to lose!

SHOTWELL PUBLISHING

Southern Without Apology.

Printed in Great Britain
by Amazon